Doomed History

SUNKEN SHIP OF DREAMS!

The *Titanic*, 1912

by Anne O'Daly

Bearport Publishing

Minneapolis, Minnesota

Picture Credits: Front Cover, ©Max Dannenbaum/Getty Images; 1, ©Library of Congress; 3, ©FLHC U1/Alamy; 4, ©Shawshots/Alamy; 5, ©Archive PL/Alamy; 7r, ©Shawshots/Alamy; 7b, ©Robert Welch/nmni.com/Harland and Wolff collection/Public Domain; 8, ©Library of Congress; 9, ©Engineering Journal/The White Star Liner Titanic, Vol.91/Public Domain; 10, ©GL Archive/Alamy; 11, ©Serban Bogdan/Shutterstock; 12–13, ©INTERFOTO/Alamy; 14, ©Oksana Shchelkanova/Shutterstock; 15, ©Photo 12/Alamy; 16, ©Francis Browne/Public Domain; 17, ©Llcentury/Public Domain; 18–19, ©Library of Congress; 20, ©CloudContrast/iStock; 21, ©World History Archive/Alamy; 22, ©National Archives; 23, ©Library of Congress; 24–25, © Shawshots/Alamy; 25, ©Library of Congress; 26, ©FAY 2018/Alamy; 26–27, ©Coast Guard Visual Information Gallery/USCG Ice Patrol/U.S. Government/Public Domain; 28, ©Library of Congress; 29, ©NOAA.

Bearport Publishing Company Product Development Team
President: Jen Jenson; Director of Product Development: Spencer Brinker; Senior Editor: Allison Juda; Editor: Charly Haley; Associate Editor: Naomi Reich; Senior Designer: Colin O'Dea; Associate Designer: Elena Klinkner; Product Development Assistant: Anita Stasson

Brown Bear Books
Children's Publisher: Anne O'Daly; Design Manager: Keith Davis;
Picture Manager: Sophie Mortimer

Library of Congress Cataloging-in-Publication Data is available at www.loc.gov or upon request from the publisher.

ISBN: 979-8-88509-084-1 (hardcover)
ISBN: 979-8-88509-091-9 (paperback)
ISBN: 979-8-88509-098-8 (ebook)

© 2023 Brown Bear Books
This edition is published by arrangement with Brown Bear Books.

North American adaptations © 2023 Bearport Publishing Company. All rights reserved. No part of this publication may be reproduced in whole or in part, stored in any retrieval system, or transmitted in any form or by any means, electronic, mechanical, photocopying, recording, or otherwise, without written permission from the publisher.

For more information, write to Bearport Publishing, 5357 Penn Avenue South, Minneapolis, MN 55419.

CONTENTS

The Ship of Dreams 4
The First Signs of Trouble 6
Disaster Strikes 12
Life or Death 18
What Happened Next 24

Key Dates 30
Quiz 30
Glossary 31
Index 32
Read More 32
Learn More Online 32

―― April 10, 1912 ――

THE SHIP OF DREAMS

The *Titanic* set sail for its first voyage on April 10, 1912. It was the largest and most **luxurious** ship on the seas. But the ship would never reach its destination.

The new ocean **liner** was docked in Southampton, England, and there was buzz all around as the ship was getting ready for its **maiden voyage**. The last of the supplies were loaded as crew members made the final preparations to cross the ocean.

Posters advertised the ship's maiden voyage.

The *Titanic* waits to leave the dock at Southampton. It would never return.

All Aboard

The ship's passengers began arriving. They included everyday travelers as well as millionaires and **aristocrats**. Also on the ship was J. Bruce Ismay, whose family ran the White Star Line—the company that owned the *Titanic*. Soon, the ship's loud whistles sounded. It was time to leave. As **tugs** pulled the *Titanic* out of the docks, another ship drifted toward it. Only the captain's quick thinking prevented a collision. Was this a hint of the disaster that was to come?

— April 11-14, 1912 —

THE FIRST SIGNS OF TROUBLE

The ship took on more passengers in France and Ireland. It left Ireland on April 11 and was due to reach New York on April 17.

As the ship sped across the Atlantic Ocean, its passengers settled in for the journey. Their experiences could be very different depending on how wealthy they were. The ship was divided into three classes. The top decks were for wealthy first-class passengers. They could spend their days in a well-stocked library, a gym, and a grand dining room.

ALL ABOARD
* Ship's capacity: 3,300 people
* Number of crew: 908
* Number of passengers: 1,317
* First class: 324
* Second class: 284
* Third class: 709

Second and Third Class

The second-class passengers had access to a smoking room, library, and dining room. The poorest passengers traveled in third class, or **steerage**. Their **cabins** were deep below deck on the lowest levels. Single men in steerage were kept at one end of the ship, while women and families were at the other. There were just two bathtubs for more than 700 third-class passengers. Many in steerage were from poor countries and were going to America to start a new life.

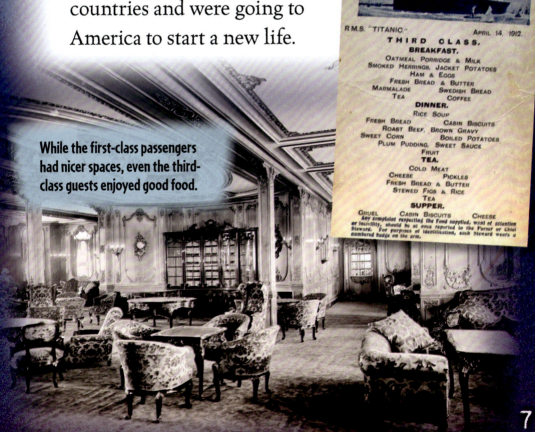

While the first-class passengers had nicer spaces, even the third-class guests enjoyed good food.

Building the Boat

The *Titanic*'s story had started three years earlier. Construction began on March 31, 1909, in Belfast, Ireland—a city well-known for ship building. The new ship was made using the best materials available. Its outer covering, or **hull**, was made from sheets of steel that were 1 inch (25 mm) thick. The ship also had a double-layered bottom.

More than 15,000 people helped construct the *Titanic*. It took over two years to build the massive ship.

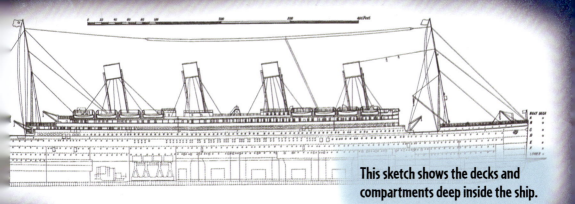

This sketch shows the decks and compartments deep inside the ship.

Bulkheads

The *Titanic* was built to be unsinkable. Its hull was divided into 16 **compartments**, each separated by walls called **bulkheads**. If a compartment had a leak, the bulkhead could be closed to contain any water coming in. The ship would still float even if four compartments were flooded. But there was a flaw in the design. The bulkheads didn't reach all the way to the ceiling. If one compartment overflowed, water could still spill into the next, even after the bulkhead was closed.

LIFEBOATS

The ship had only 20 lifeboats for the 2,225 people on board. This was partly because the designers of the ship didn't think it could ever sink. Another reason was that lifeboats took up space, and the owners wanted to give passengers a lot of room to relax on deck.

Ice Warnings

Sunday, April 14 started sunny but cold. The sea was calm, and the ship was making good progress. It was traveling at a rate of 22 **knots** (25 miles per hour, or 40 kph). At that speed, the *Titanic* might reach New York a day early. The ship had received warnings from others in the area about ice, but this was not uncommon. Captain Smith changed his course slightly but didn't slow down. Urged on by Ismay, Smith wanted to show how fast the ship was.

CAPTAIN SMITH

Captain Edward J. Smith was an experienced sailor. He joined the White Star Line in 1886 and had been in charge of a number of their ships. After a long career, Smith planned to retire when he finished the *Titanic's* maiden voyage. At the time of the crash, he was asleep in his cabin.

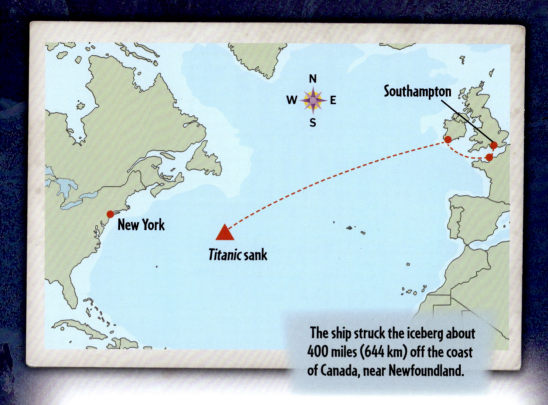

The ship struck the iceberg about 400 miles (644 km) off the coast of Canada, near Newfoundland.

"Iceberg Right Ahead!"

That evening, the two officers on **watch** were looking at the open seas without the usual help from their binoculars, which had been lost. At about 11:40 p.m., one of the men spotted a huge iceberg dangerously close to the ship. He signalled the **bridge** and shouted "Iceberg right ahead!" Officers tried to steer the ship away from the floating ice, but the Titanic was moving too fast to make the turn. The ship's right side scraped along the iceberg.

— April 14, 1912 —

DISASTER STRIKES

Captain Smith was woken by the sound of the collision. He headed to the bridge. Chief engineer Thomas Andrews went to inspect the damage.

The crash had **punctured** the first six compartments in the hull, and the *Titanic* was now filling with water. Andrews told Captain Smith the bad news—the ship had less than two hours before it would sink into the icy water.

Lowering the Lifeboats

Captain Smith told the crew to get the lifeboats ready. By then, passengers were pouring onto the deck, scared and confused. People didn't know what to do. Officers told women and children to get into the lifeboats first. The crew started to lower lifeboats into the water. But some of the boats were only half full as they left the ship. Many people were still stuck on the sinking *Titanic*.

The *Titanic*'s lifeboats had space for 1,178 people. But only 706 were saved.

Boats still use signal rockets to call for help when they are in trouble.

Shots Fired

Officers fired signal rockets into the air as they were loading the lifeboats. They hoped those left onboard would be saved by another nearby ship. But the *Titanic* continued to sink lower. Its **stern** tipped up into the air. Passengers stranded on the boat panicked as the last lifeboats were lowered into the water below.

Lost Down Below

Steerage passengers had to climb up from the lower decks to reach the lifeboats that were kept on the upper decks. Many became trapped as the ship filled with water. Although almost two-thirds of first-class passengers survived the disaster, only a quarter of third-class passengers did.

THE BAND PLAYED ON

While passengers climbed into the lifeboats, the Titanic's band played popular songs and happy tunes to keep everyone calm. Later, as the situation became hopeless, they played religious hymns. The musicians kept playing as long as they could. Each of them went down with the ship.

The brave musicians played to the sinking passengers as the lifeboats were lowered away.

Before the accident, Harold Bride (*pictured*) and Jack Phillips were busy sending **telegrams** for the wealthy passengers.

Sending Messages

The *Titanic*'s had one last hope. At 12:15 a.m. the ship's two radio operators were told to send distress signals to anybody who could hear them. The chief operator, Jack Phillips, and his assistant, Harold Bride, sent out the desperate messages.

Calls for Help

The operators sent calls for help to every ship within range. They continued sending messages until the ship's power was gone. Bride was later swept off the ship into the ocean, but he managed to climb into a lifeboat and survive. Phillips was still sending calls for help as the radio room filled with water. He went down with the ship.

Jack Phillips was nicknamed Sparks for his skill and speed at sending messages.

April 15, 1912
LIFE OR DEATH

The survivors in the lifeboats were frightened and confused. Many had left family on the ship that they would never see again.

The *Titanic*'s lifeboats rowed away quickly. By 2:05 a.m., the ship's **bow** was completely underwater, and its stern was sticking up in the air. One of the ship's giant chimney-like funnels collapsed and fell into the sea, crushing several passengers.

The survivors on the lifeboats knew the sinking ship would suck down anything nearby when it finally went under.

Breaking Apart

At 2:12 a.m., the giant ocean liner let out four loud bangs. Shortly after, at 2:18 a.m., the ship's lights went out. With a loud wrenching sound, the *Titanic* broke into two pieces. It then sank into the dark, icy water.

Last Moments

There were still more than a thousand people on the ship as it sank. Many jumped into the water and held on to floating **debris**, but others were sucked down with the ship. Some tried to swim to the lifeboats, but they were too far away. The water was so cold that a person could survive for only about 20 minutes before dying of **hypothermia**.

Only one-tenth of an iceberg is visible above the surface of the water.

ICEBERGS

Icebergs are giant blocks of ice that float in the ocean. They break off from larger glaciers. Arctic icebergs, like the one that sank the Titanic, can be as big as a 10-story building. Most of their size is hidden under the water.

Members of the crew in their life jackets. There were 908 crew members on board. Only 212 of them survived.

Haunting Cries

The people in the lifeboats could hear desperate cries for help all around them, a sound that haunted the survivors for the rest of their lives. Most of the people in the lifeboats worried the boats would sink if they had too many people in them. Only two of the lifeboats went back to try and rescue survivors from the water.

Help Arrives

About half an hour after the *Titanic* sunk, the cries of the passengers in the water faded away. But for the survivors in the lifeboats, help was on its way. A ship called the *Carpathia* had picked up a distress signal and raced to help the *Titanic*. The *Carpathia* arrived at 3:30 a.m. Its crew began looking desperately for survivors.

This lifeboat was photographed by a sailor from the deck of the *Carpathia*.

On the *Carpathia*, survivors were given blankets as well as hot food and drinks.

Rescue!

Just after 4:00 a.m., the *Carpathia* spotted the first survivors. It spent the next four hours rescuing passengers on the lifeboats. As they rowed to the *Carpathia*, many survivors cheered. Others were silent with shock and grief. By about 9:00 a.m., 705 of the *Titanic*'s passengers were safely on the *Carpathia*. No other survivors were found.

— 1912 and later —

WHAT HAPPENED NEXT

The sinking of the Titanic shocked the world. People made new rules to stop any future disasters at sea.

With its new passengers on board, the *Carpathia* set off for New York. Its radio operators sent ahead a list with the names of the survivors, and Ismay sent a telegram to the White Star offices to tell them the tragic news. Slowly, the story of the *Titanic* spread. Early reports said that all the passengers were safe. But gradually, the awful truth came out.

People learned about the size of the disaster from newspapers.

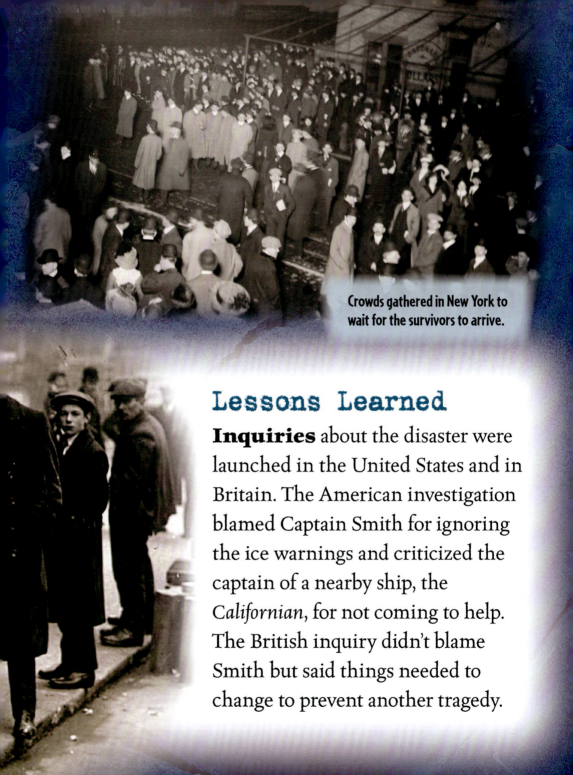

Crowds gathered in New York to wait for the survivors to arrive.

Lessons Learned

Inquiries about the disaster were launched in the United States and in Britain. The American investigation blamed Captain Smith for ignoring the ice warnings and criticized the captain of a nearby ship, the *Californian*, for not coming to help. The British inquiry didn't blame Smith but said things needed to change to prevent another tragedy.

The American inquiry began in New York on April 19, 1912.

Changes in the Law

The inquires led to new laws. All ships would now have to carry enough lifeboats for every person on board. There had to be regular **drills** so people would know what to do in case of an emergency. Ships would now need a telegraph operator on duty at all times.

THE CALIFORNIAN

Both inquiries criticized the captain of a nearby ship, the *Californian*. Officers on board saw rockets coming from the *Titanic*, but the captain didn't think they were warning signals. The *Californian*'s radio operator had finished work for the night and didn't pick up the *Titanic*'s distress signals until the next day.

International Ice Patrol

The disaster also sparked the formation of the International Ice Patrol. Run by the U.S. Coast Guard and based in Newfoundland, Canada, the patrol has two airplanes, and their pilots keep an eye out for icebergs. If any large pieces of ice are getting close to shipping lanes, the patrol warns passing ships.

The International Ice Patrol collects information about icebergs and sends it to nearby ships.

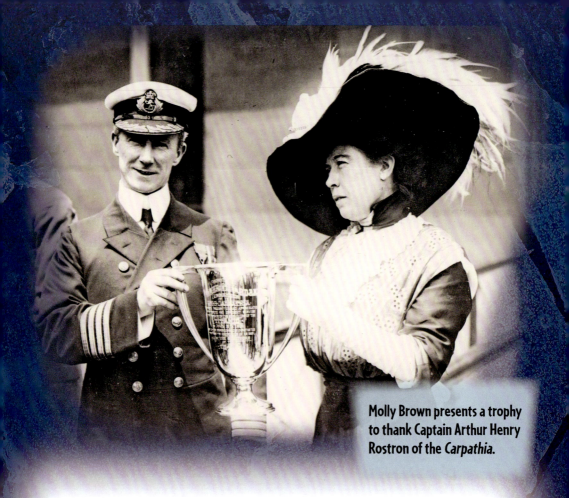

Molly Brown presents a trophy to thank Captain Arthur Henry Rostron of the *Carpathia*.

Acts of Bravery

Dramatic accounts from survivors appeared in newspapers around the world. One of the survivors was an American millionaire named Molly Brown. As the *Titanic* sank, she helped others into the lifeboats. She also took charge of her lifeboat and rowed toward the rescue ship. Brown later headed a group that raised money for survivors of the disaster.

Finding the Ship

The Titanic's **wreck** remained undiscovered until 1985 when American **oceanographer** Dr. Robert Ballard found it. He sent a remote-controlled **submarine** to take pictures of what was left of the ship. Since then, other groups have explored the ship, too. For more than one hundred years, the world has remembered the ship that took so many to their watery grave.

In 1985, Dr. Ballard's team photographed the Titanic where it rests on the seabed, nearly 2 miles (3 km) below the surface.

KEY DATES

March 31, 1909 The construction of the *Titanic* begins

1912

April 10 The ship leaves Southampton on its maiden voyage; it stops at France and Ireland

April 11 The *Titanic* sets sail for America

April 14

morning Officers receive ice warnings from nearby ships

5:50 p.m. Captain Smith changes course but does not slow down

11:40 p.m. A lookout spots an iceberg. The *Titanic* turns, but hits the iceberg. The ship begins to take on water.

April 15

12:15 a.m. *Titanic* sends out distress signals

12:25 a.m. The *Carpathia* hears distress signals and races to the rescue

4:10 a.m. The *Carpathia* starts picking up survivors

April 18 The *Carpathia* reaches New York

April 19–May 25 American inquiry into the disaster

May 2–July 3 British inquiry

1985 Dr. Robert Ballard discovers the *Titanic*'s wreck

QUIZ

How much have you learned about the *Titanic* disaster? It's time to test your knowledge! Then, check your answers on page 32.

1. **What was the company that owned the *Titanic*?**
   a) Blue Diamond Line
   b) White Star Line
   c) Purple Circle Line

2. **How many lifeboats were on the ship?**
   a) 20
   b) 150
   c) 300

3. **Where was Captain Smith when the ship hit the iceberg?**
   a) on the bridge
   b) in his cabin
   c) in the library

4. **What was telegraph operator Jack Phillips' nickname?**
   a) Speedy
   b) Words
   c) Sparks

5. **What was the name of the ship that rescued the survivors?**
   a) the *Carpathia*
   b) the *Californian*
   c) the *Canadian*

GLOSSARY

aristocrats people who belong to the upper classes of society

bow the front of a ship or boat

bridge the front part of a ship from where the captain and other officers steer the ship

bulkheads walls in a ship's hull

cabins rooms on a ship where passengers sleep

compartments seperated areas of a train, boat, or plane

debris the pieces left over when something has been destroyed

drills training exercises

hull the body of a ship or boat

hypothermia an extremely dangerous condition in which a person's body temperature drops to be extremely low

inquiries official studies held by experts to find out the facts about disasters

knots the unit that measures a ship's speed

liner a large ship that carries passengers along fixed routes, or lines

luxurious very comfortable, fancy, and expensive

maiden voyage a ship's first journey

oceanographer a scientist who studies oceans

punctured made a hole in something

steerage the cheapest type of passenger cabin or room on a ship

stern the back of a ship or boat

submarine a ship that is designed to travel underwater

telegrams messages sent over long distances by radio

tugs small, powerful boats used for towing larger boats and ships

watch the act of staying awake to keep guard or to keep on the lookout for danger

wreck the remains of a ship that has been badly damaged or destroyed

INDEX

Andrews, Thomas 12
Ballard, Robert 29–30
band 15
Brown, Molly 28
bulkheads 9
Californian, the 25–26, 30
Carpathia, the 22–24, 28, 30
construction 8, 30
first class 6–7, 15
iceberg 11, 20, 27, 30
inquiries 25–26, 30
Ismay, J. Bruce 5, 10, 24–25
lifeboat drills 26
maiden voyage 4, 10, 30
New York 6, 10–11, 24–26, 30
second class 6–7
Southampton 4–5, 11, 13, 30
steerage class 7, 15
survivors 18, 21–25, 28, 30
telegraph 16, 26, 30
White Star Line 5, 10, 24, 30
wreck 29–30

READ MORE

Messner, Kate. *The Titanic* (*History Smashers*). New York: Random House, 2021.

Montero, Mary. *Titanic Q&A: 100+ Fascinating Facts for Kids* (*History Q&A*). Emeryville, CA: Rockridge Press, 2020.

Oachs, Emily Rose. *Titanic* (*Torque: Digging up the Past*). Minneapolis, MN: Bellwether Media, Inc., 2020.

LEARN MORE ONLINE

1. Go to **www.factsurfer.com** or scan the QR code below.
2. Enter **"Sunken Ship"** into the search box.
3. Click on the cover of this book to see a list of websites.

Answers to the quiz on page 30

Answers: 1) B; 2) A; 3) B; 4) C; 5) A